FANCY DRESSED ANIMALS

Brian W. Parker

Edited by Sean Fishback

Copyright © 2018 Believe In Wonder Publishing, LLC/
Brian W. Parker and Josie A. Parker
Published through Amazon Createspace

All rights reserved. Published in the United States by
Believe In Wonder Publishing, Gresham, OR.

Book designed and illustration by Brian W. Parker, BFA, MA
Edited by Sean Fishback
Inside text set in Felix Tiling and Danielle
BIW "reading boy" logo is a trademark of Believe In Wonder Publishing, LLC

Printed in the U.S.A
For bulk orders, event booking, and questions about publishing services,
please email us at believeinwonderpublishing@gmail.com

ISBN-13: 978-1981920457
ISBN-10: 1981920455

BISAC: Art / Individual Artists / Artists Books

First Edition

Summary: Author and illustrator, Brian W. Parker, proudly brings together a collection of skillfully executed pencil drawings depicting a menagerie of animals in fine clothing.

Believe In Wonder is a family-owned, youth focused publishing company based in Beaverton, OR. We delight in promoting imagination, inspiration, and positive thinking in kids and adults alike, and strive to bring diverse characters and new worlds to readers and art lovers everywhere.

Visit us at **believeinwonder.com** for more books, art, and event updates.

FANCY DRESSED ANIMALS

A collection of illustrations by Brian W. Parker

CONTAINING:
Bear, koala, hedgehog, ferret, pig, fox, deer, mole
and a menagerie of other varied beasts in fine attire.

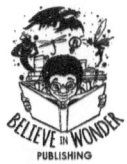

BEAVERTON • OREGON
"Wonder is the beginning of wisdom."
-Socrates

for Josie

Thank you for your patience and your support, Sweetness.

An introduction

Fancy Dressed Animals was never meant to be a book, but here it is! What started off as just a fun thought experiment for my sketch pad (a way to pass the time drawing, but not really for any particular reason) has turned into one of the most fun projects I've ever put together. I would start with an animal image, then do a little research into different forms of formal dress from the 18th and 19th centuries. Put them together along with a little imagination and some creative backstory, and you have this collection.

I hope you enjoy it.

Mr. Basha Abdu

Mr. Abdu is the owner and proprietor of Bagheera's Book Shop, and a purveyor of rare manuscripts and oddities from around the world. When he moved into the city, he was first met with skepticism because of his strange accent and cool demeanor – but quickly his neighbors and customers alike began to appreciate his keen mind, and abundant kindness to all he met.

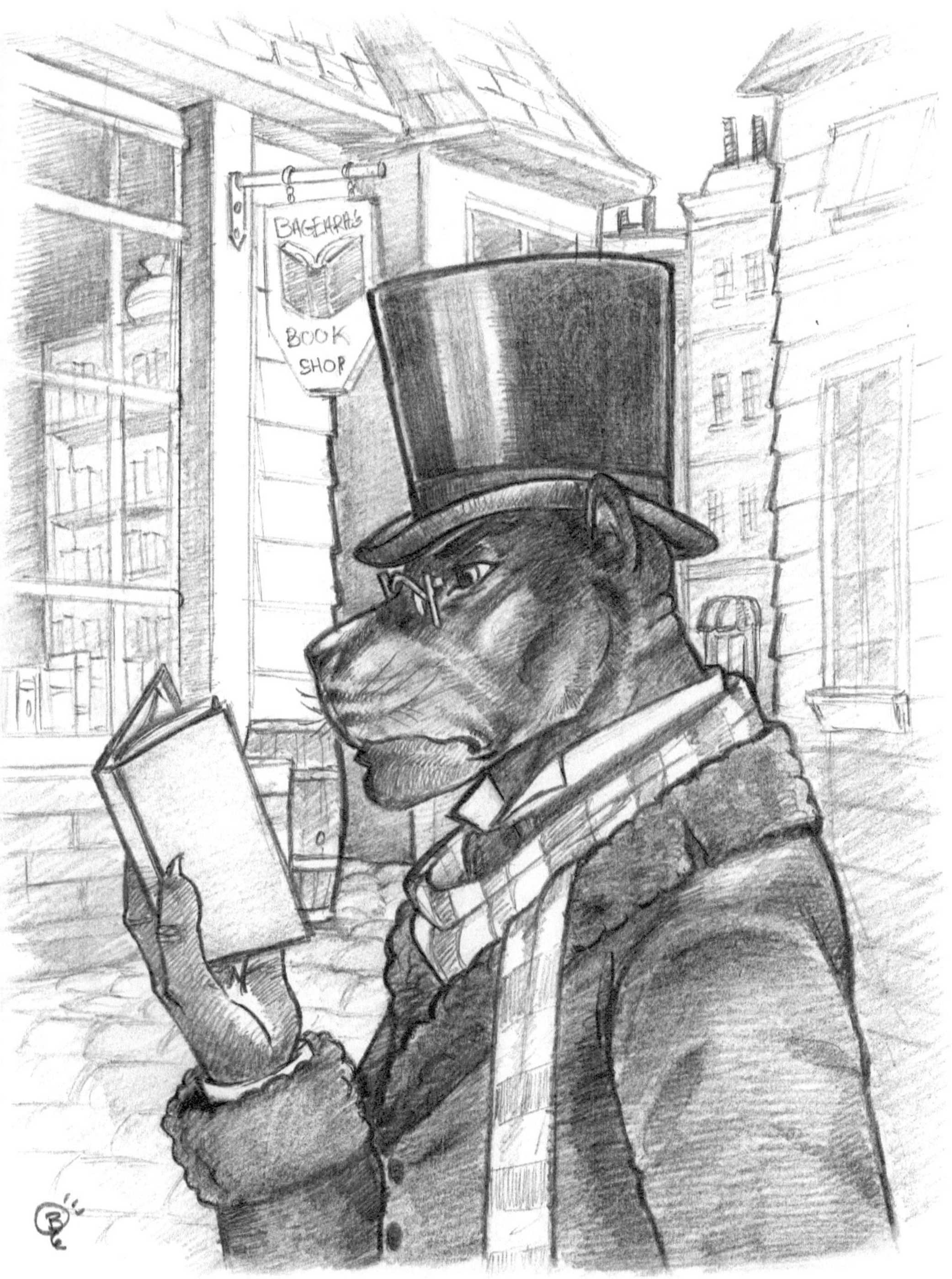

Millie Mink

An ambitious youth from the Midwest, Mildred Stoatish was determined to make a life for herself in the big city on her own terms. A regular at the jazz clubs, Millie has become a socialite of the first order – known to party goers all over as Millie Mink.

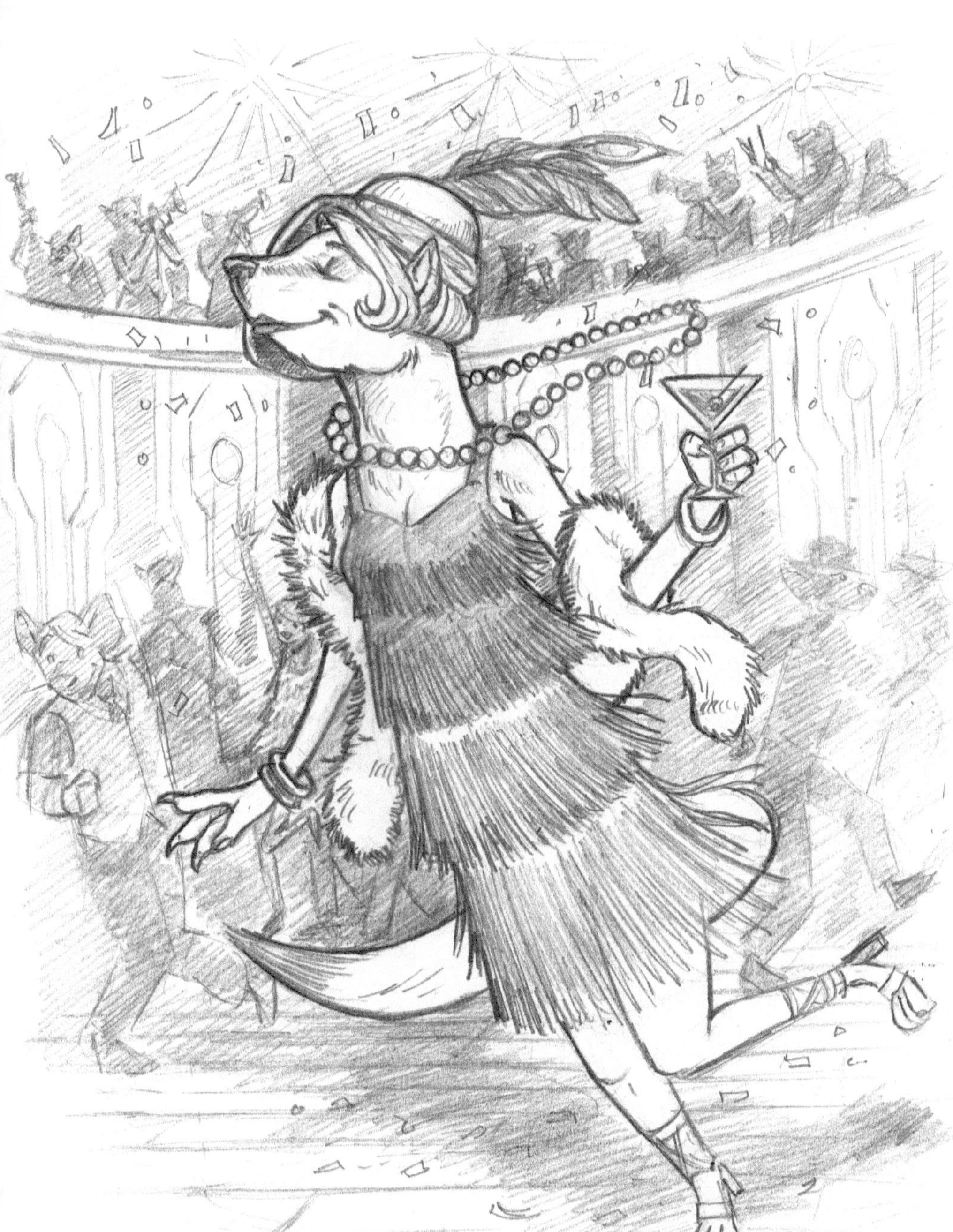

Heimish McSwine,
Lord of Loch Hampton

The land surrounding Loch Hampton is rich with culture and a thriving community of farmers in spite of the heavy-handed rule of their lord, Heimish McSwine of Clan McSwine. His family is well known for their greed and foolish pride, but Heimish is the worst in a long line of dullards. After almost choking on a chicken sandwich, he outlawed all sandwiches in the county for the afront.

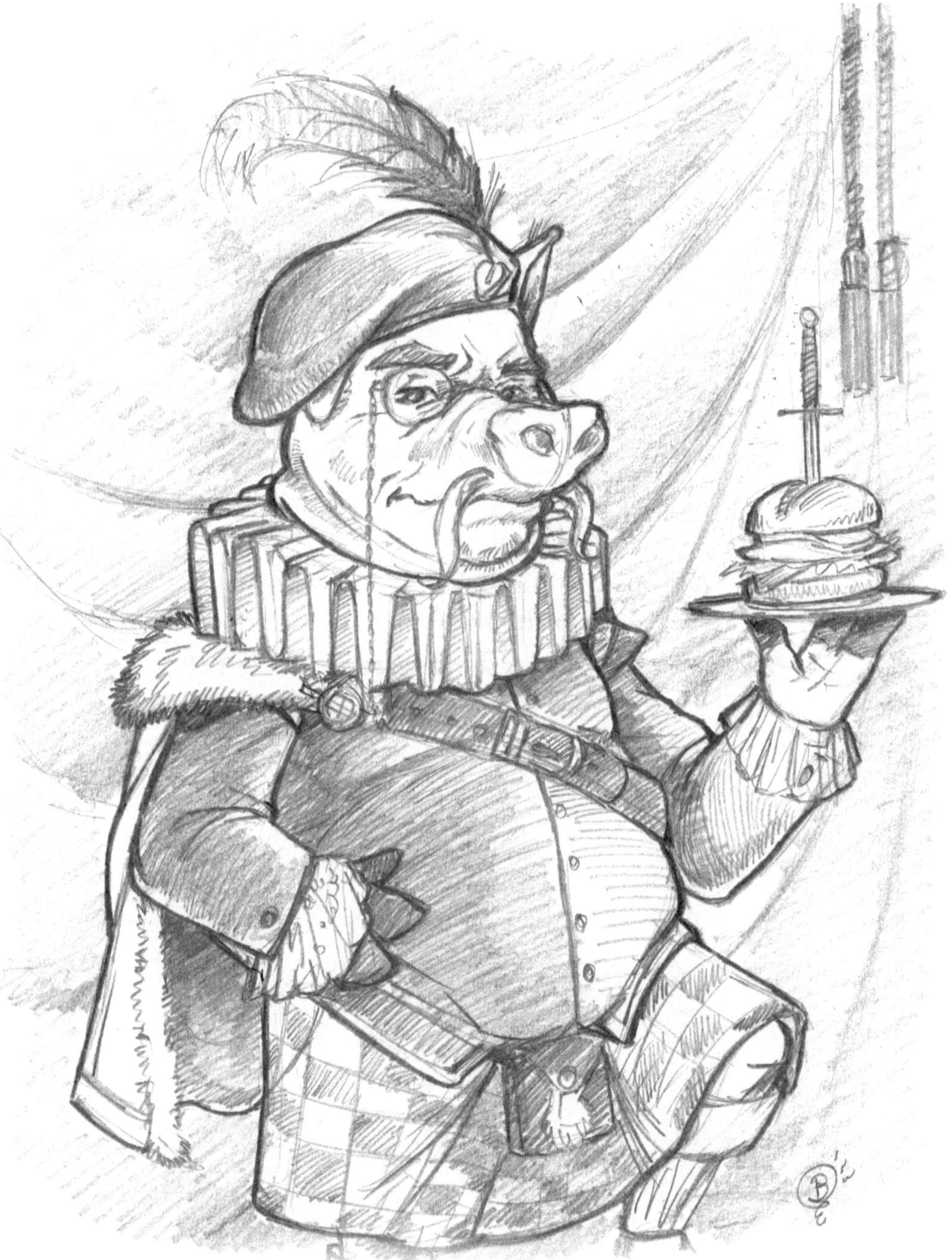

Wesley Rakoto

To some, tailoring is considered a craft, but to Wesley, it is more of a higher calling. Raised by his talented and well-respected grandmother, Mr. Rakoto learned his trade at the feet of a master who serviced the rich and those that could only pay in fruit. She was a hard teacher, never letting her grandson slack or take shortcuts. That attention to detail paid off, and now Wesley's little shop, Ring-Tails, is the bespoke tailoring establishment in the country. With that kind of notoriety, he's no longer accepting fruit in exchange for services (although, he's not above taking a nice ripe mango as a down payment.)

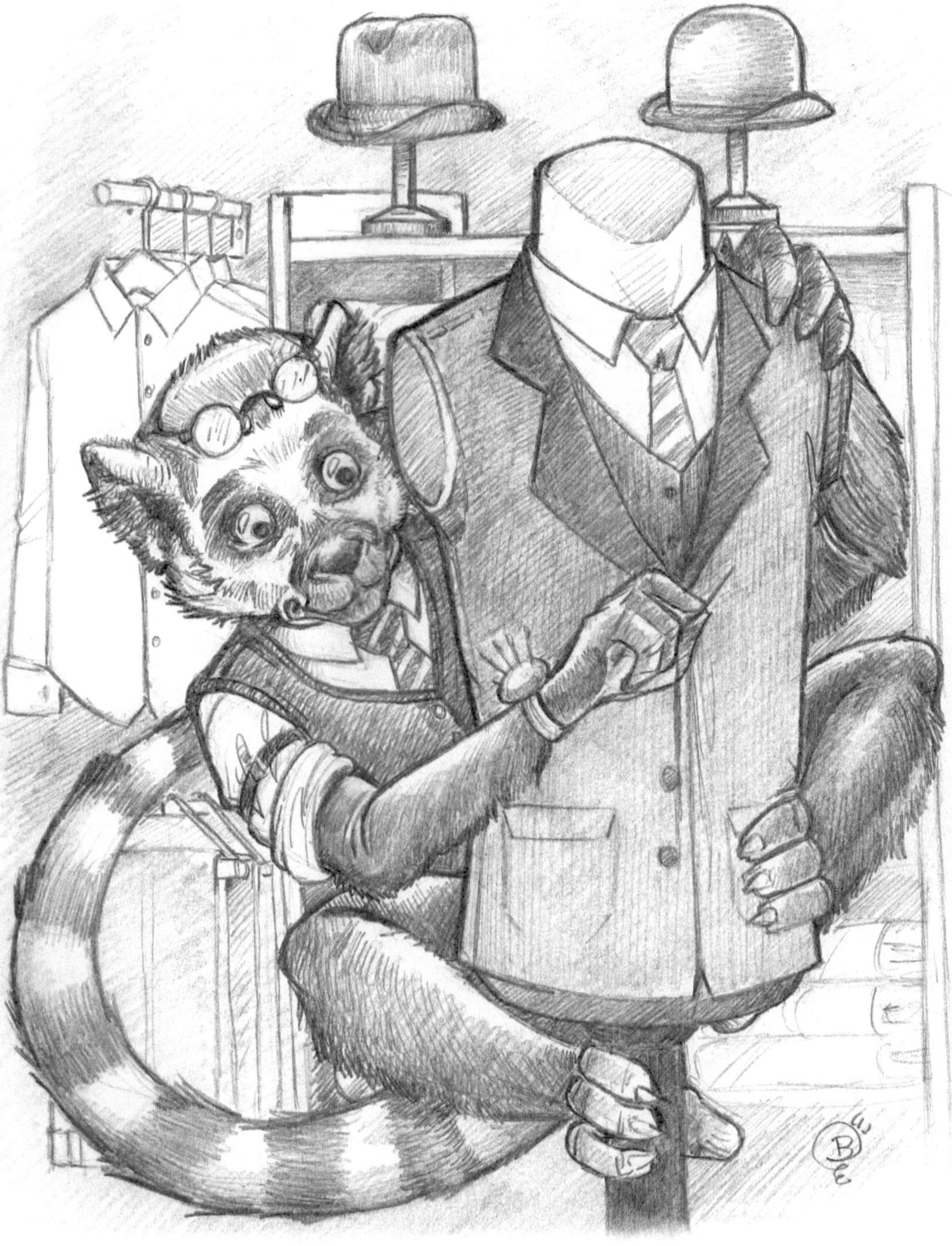

Countess Doesha de Faunico

Doesha came from humble beginnings. The daughter of the local constable, she always felt a strong responsibility to her town and neighbors. When she caught the eye of the young Count de Faunico at the annual harvest festival, and later married into his lordly family, she decided to put that sense of community responsibility to work. She had houses built for the homeless, clothed and fed the poor, and fostered education for all. She quickly became the most loved member of the de Faunico family.

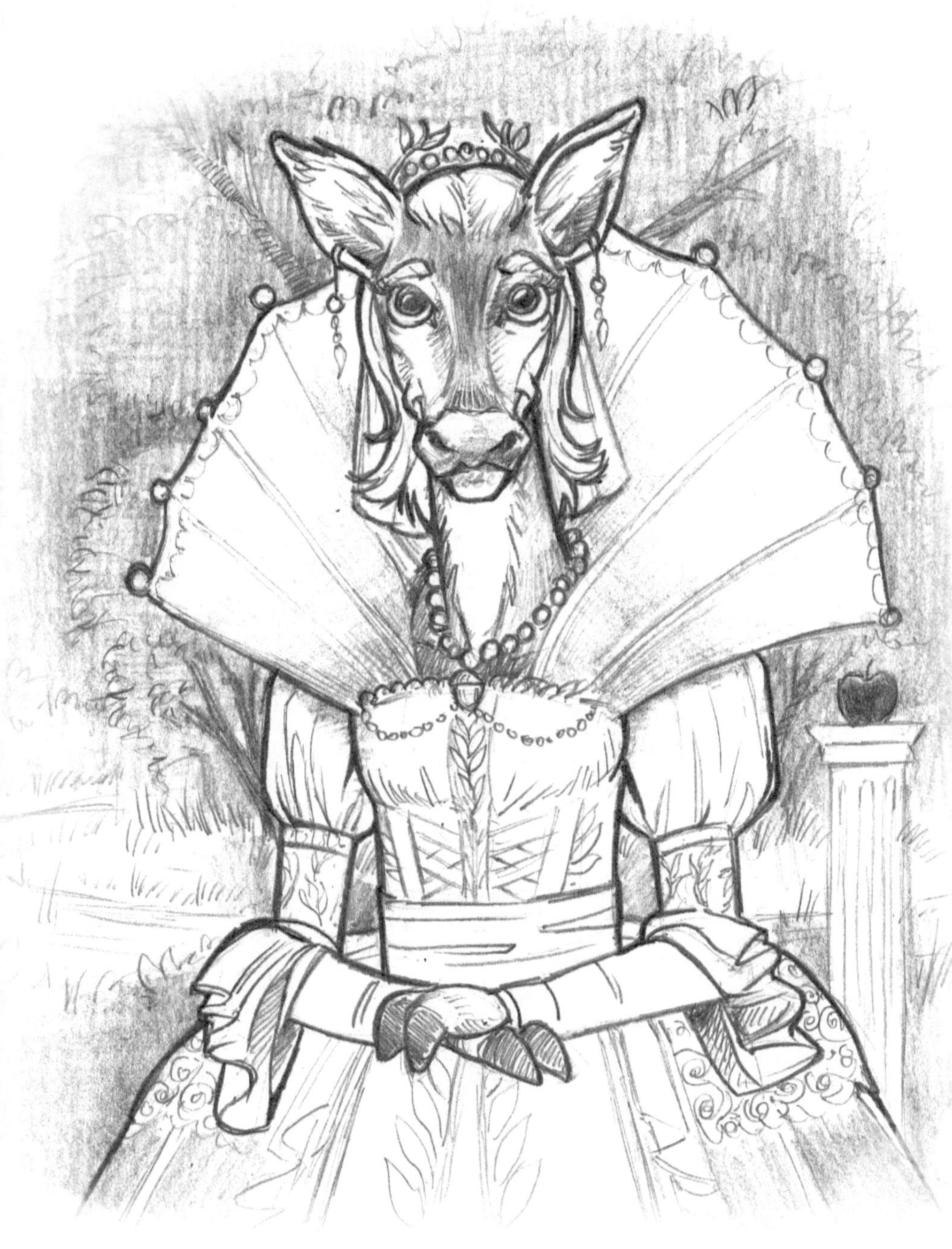

Digger VonMolert

The proprietor of VonMolert's Fine Jewelry, Digger is considered by his colleagues and customers to be the finest expert in rare gems and stones in the country. Little does the public know, he is also infamous in the world of jewel thieves, known only as The Silent Claw. Few would suspect such a mild-mannered mole of being a world-class rogue.

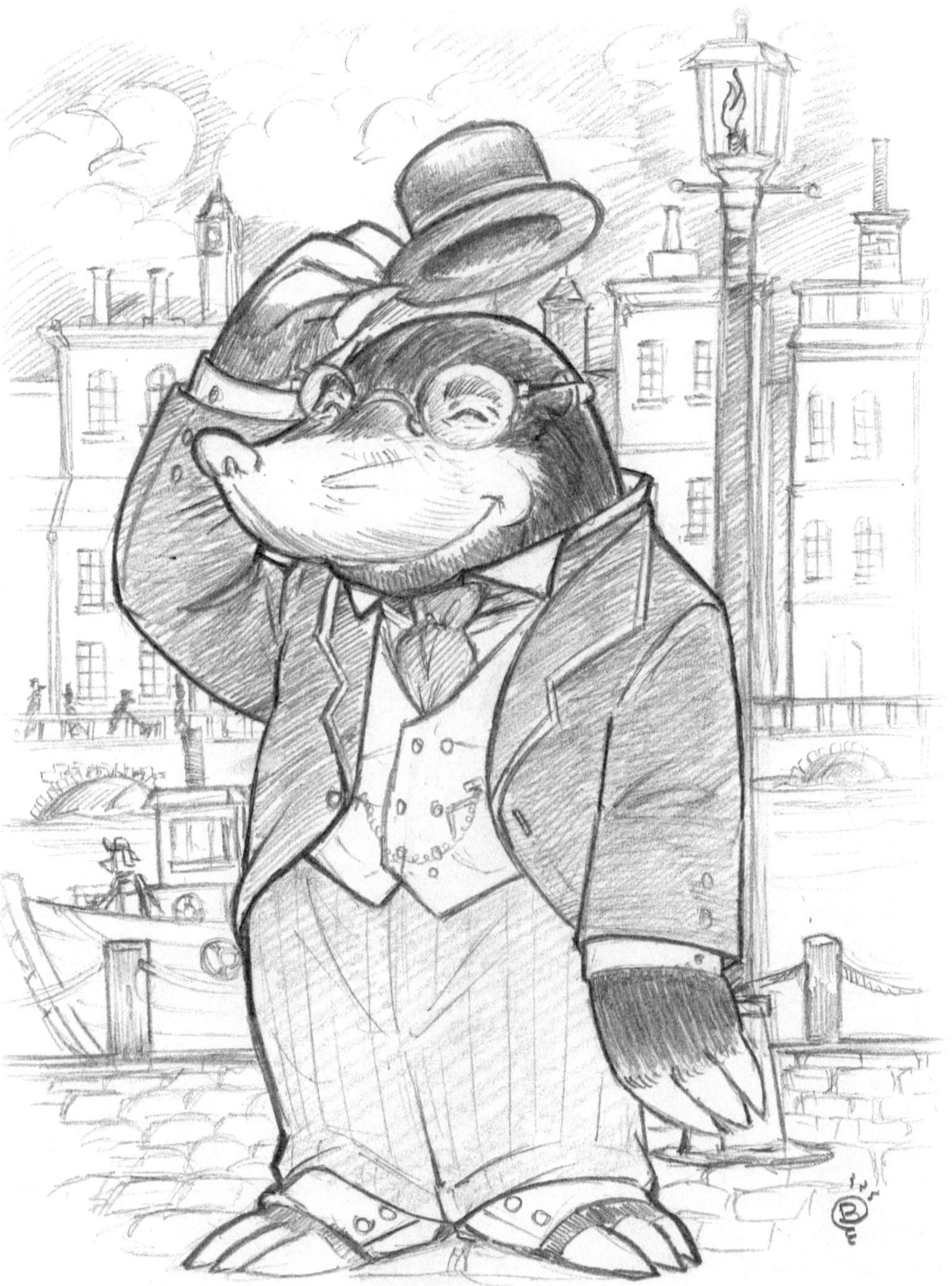

Eliza Chittering

Eliza is a fashionable young squirrel making her way at a fine nut and pastry shop, looking for Mr. Right. Always a pragmatist, Eliza is looking for a man of distinction, stature, and wealth, even though her heart belongs to poor Thomas Walton - owner of the very shop in which she works. Hopefully, love will win out over upward social mobility.

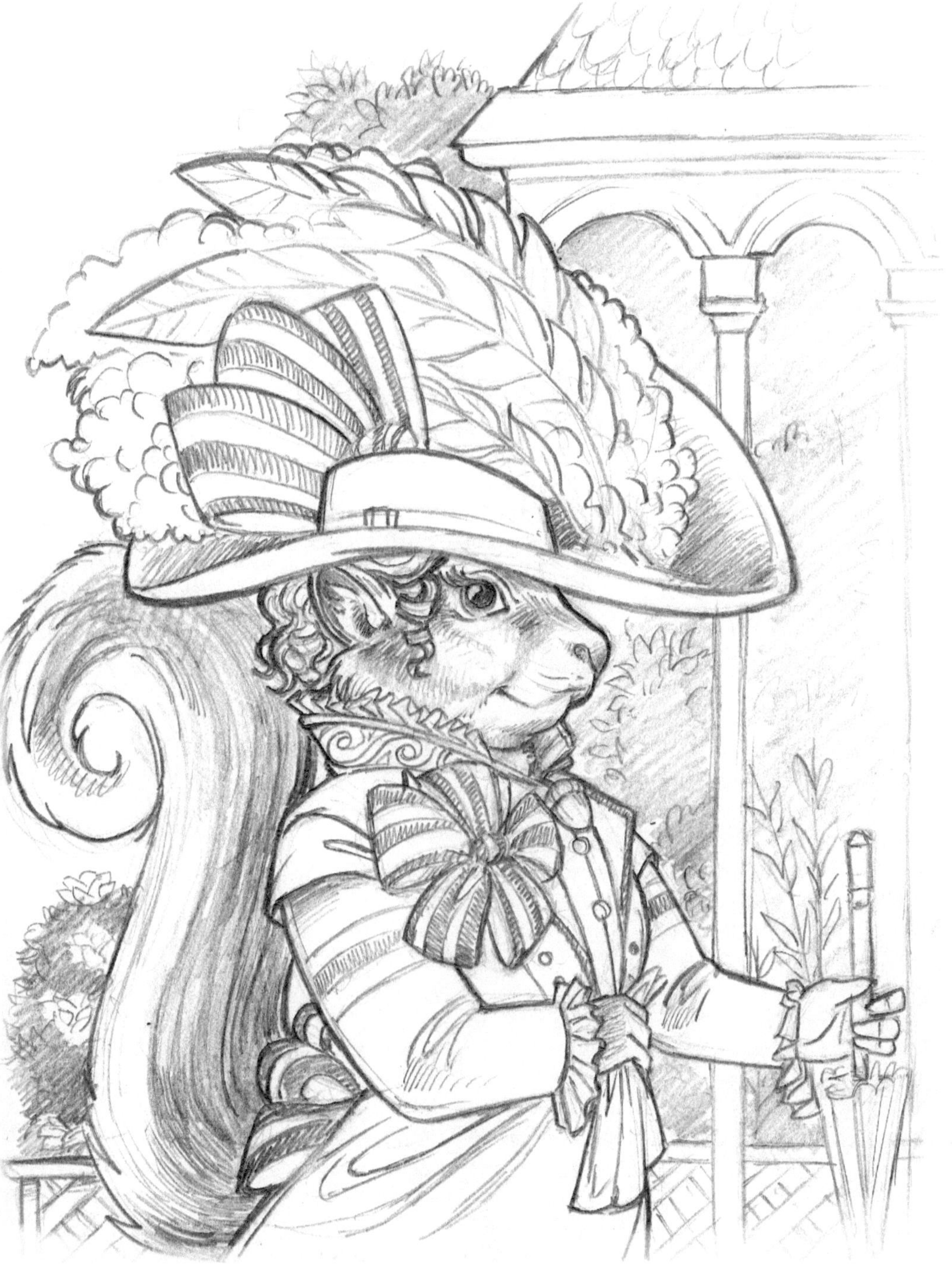

Gordon Bearington, *ESQ*

Owner of Olde Bearington's Pub, Gordon is known as Gordo to his friends, of which he has many. The pub is a favorite stop of the working crowd, but also politicians, bankers, financiers and big named mover-shakers. He welcomes them all with good food, a well-stocked bar, and the most discreet of locations to do business. It's said that the biggest deals in history have gone down under his roof, but Gordo would never confirm that. "Confidence is key," is Mr. Bearington's motto.

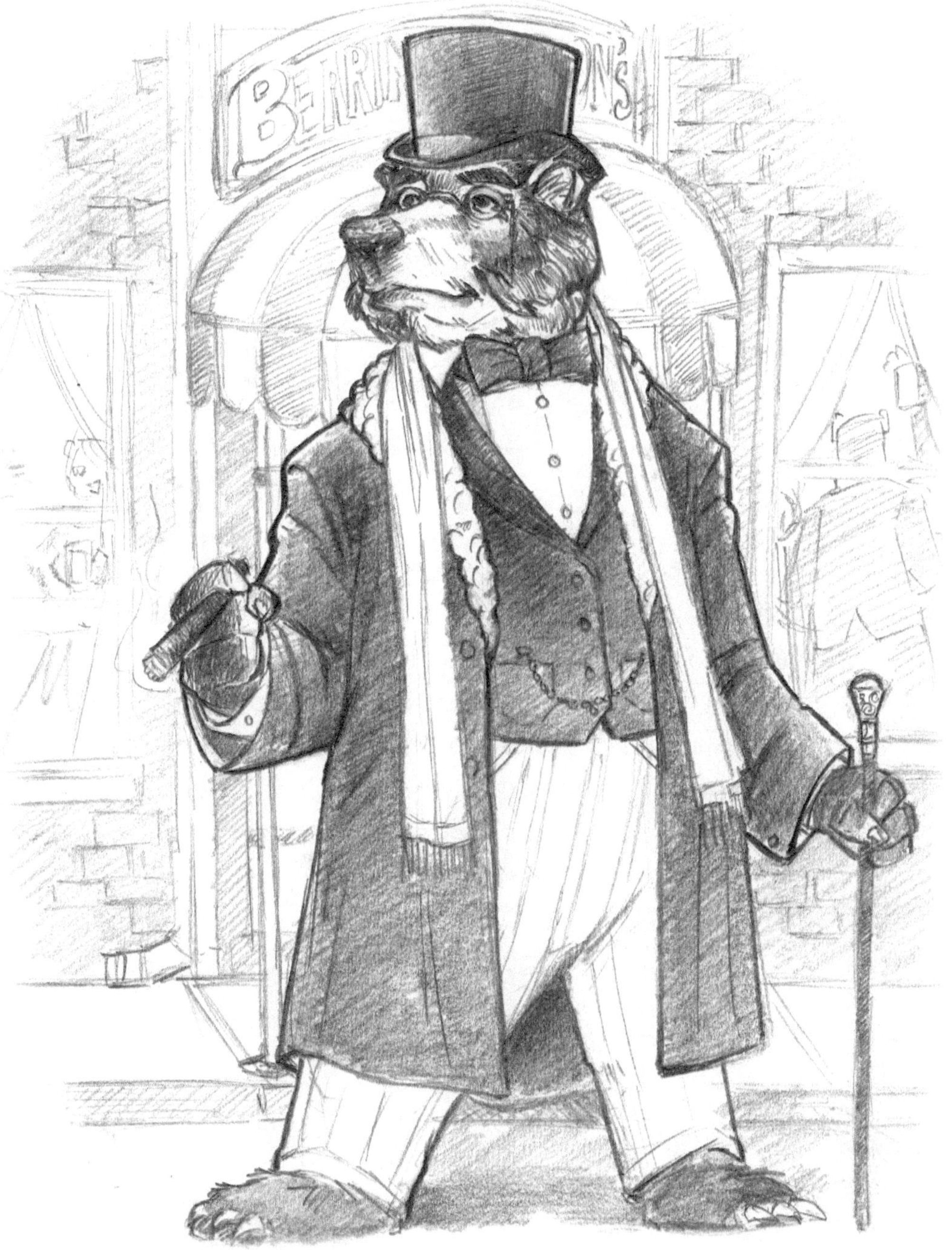

Helen Hedge Spivey

Helen is a milliner of some renown. She got her start in a little shop she purchased with the inheritance she received after marrying a traveling merchant. The coupling was short-lived (as was her husband) so she struck out on her own. Now her elaborate hats are worn by the most fashionable of ladies in high society circles. Under her sweet and demure exterior beats the heart of a true artist. She tells stories with feather and lace and a well-adorned brim. Her works are more than just accessories, they are statements.

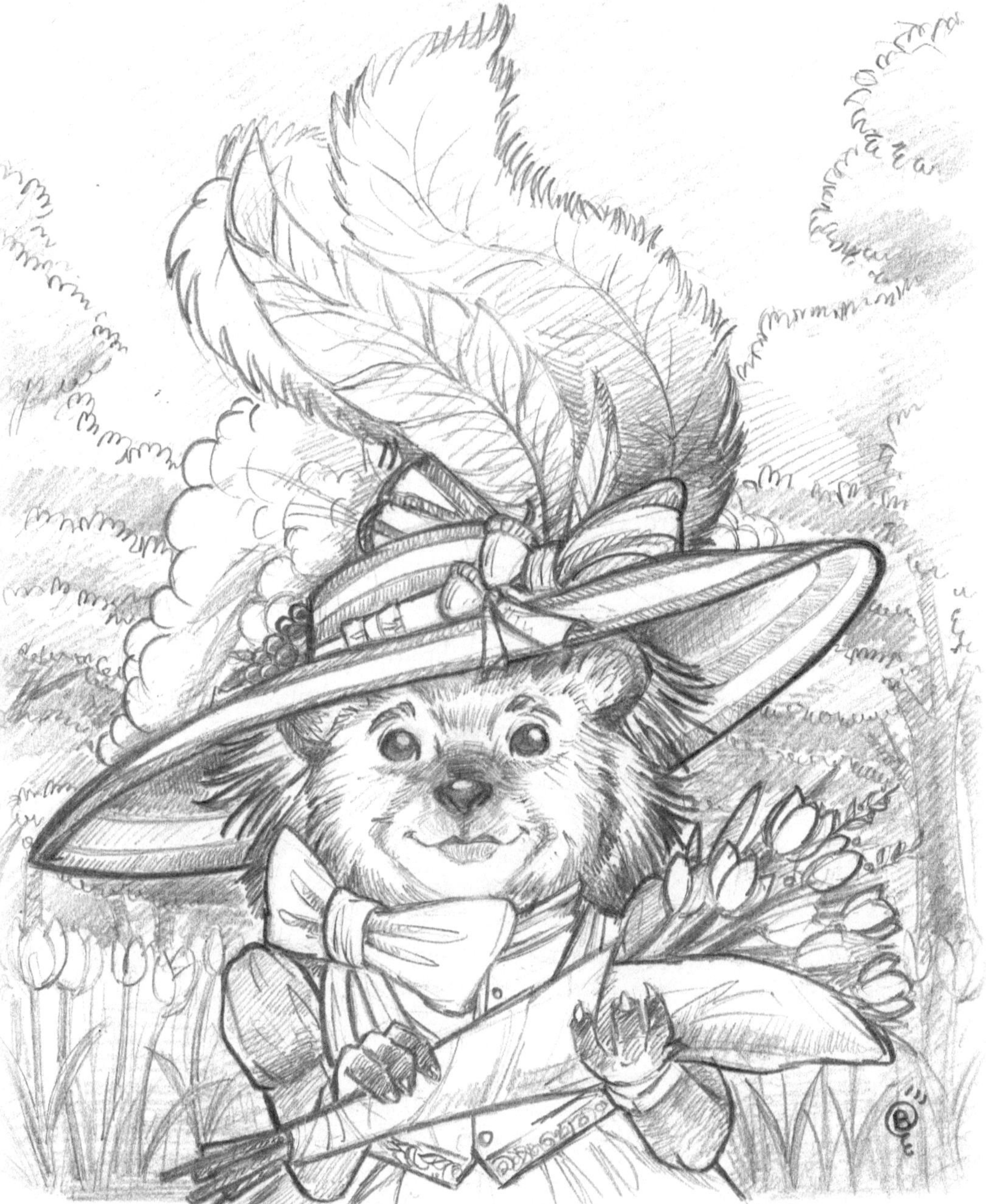

Harrington Von Hasenpfeffer

The Von Hasenpfeffer farm is known for its award-winning carrots which have been recorded to grow to the size of large children. The family has been perfecting their fertilizer for generations, and no one can quite figure out how they grow such monstrous vegetables. Some have hinted at the use of alchemy, but Harrington is tight-lipped on the subject. Whatever their secret is, the carrots are delicious.

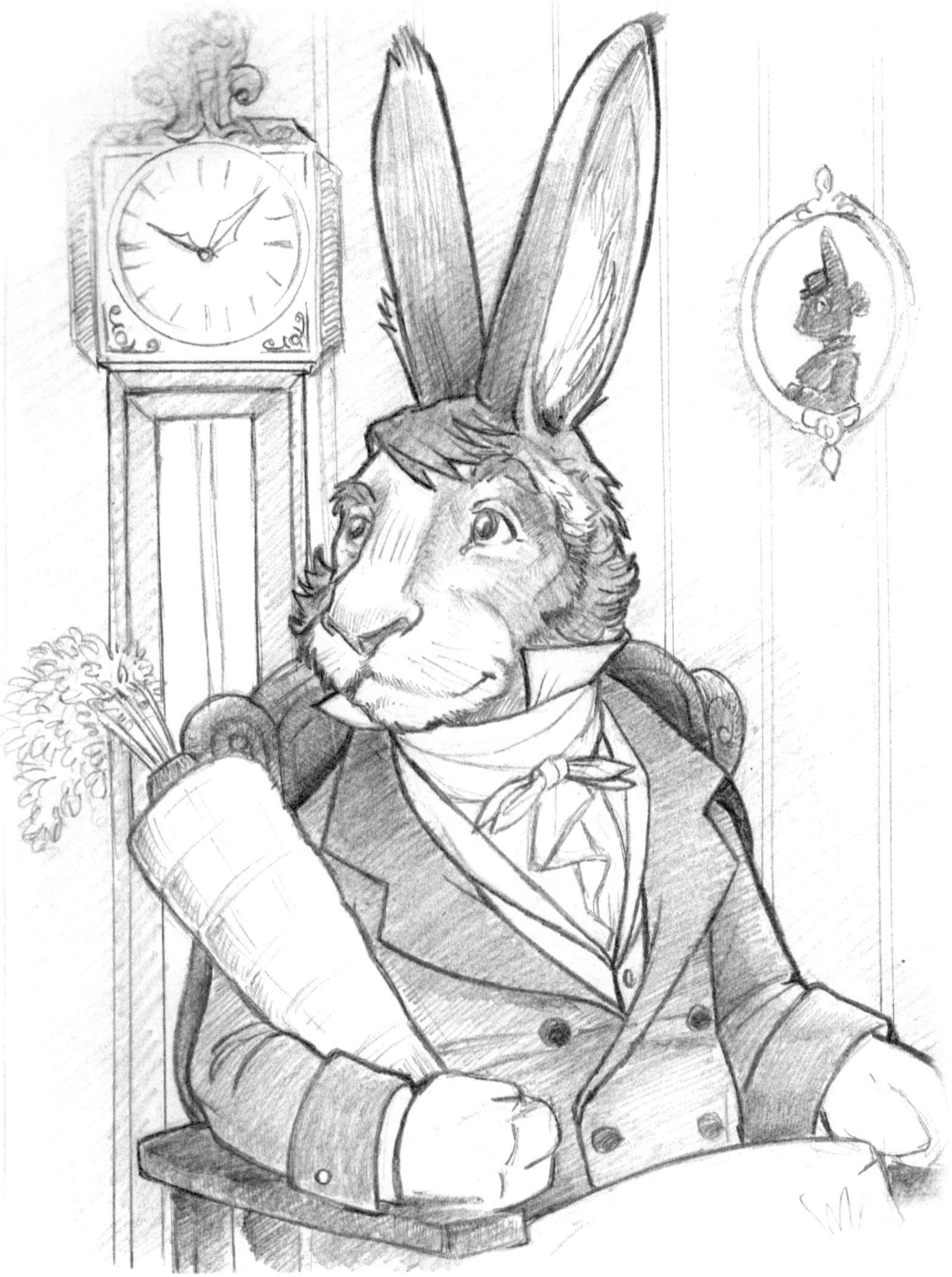

Lt. Rochford Coonatious

Although you wouldn't guess it right away, Rochford is one of the most strategically minded officers in his majesty's army. He has a penchant for starting impromptu parties and a nose for fine wines, both of which has kept him from achieving the respect of his superiors. They have, however, earned him the love of his men.

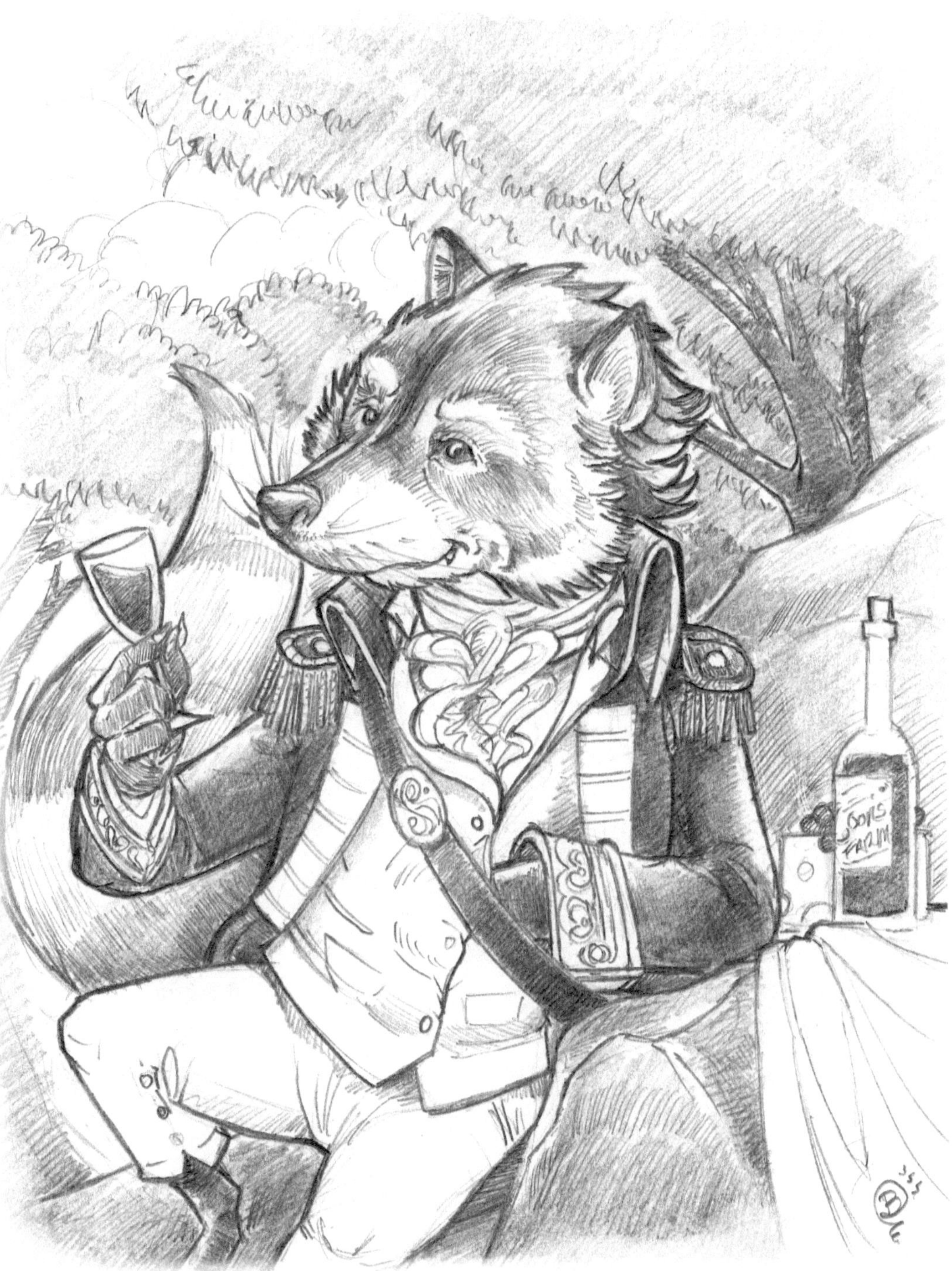

Koda O'Girdwood

Either wandering worn paths through the mountains or camping at the foot of mountains in far off places, Koda O'Girdwood is the epitome of the stately traveler and dog of leisure. He has made it his mission to see the world – at a calm and easy pace, of course.

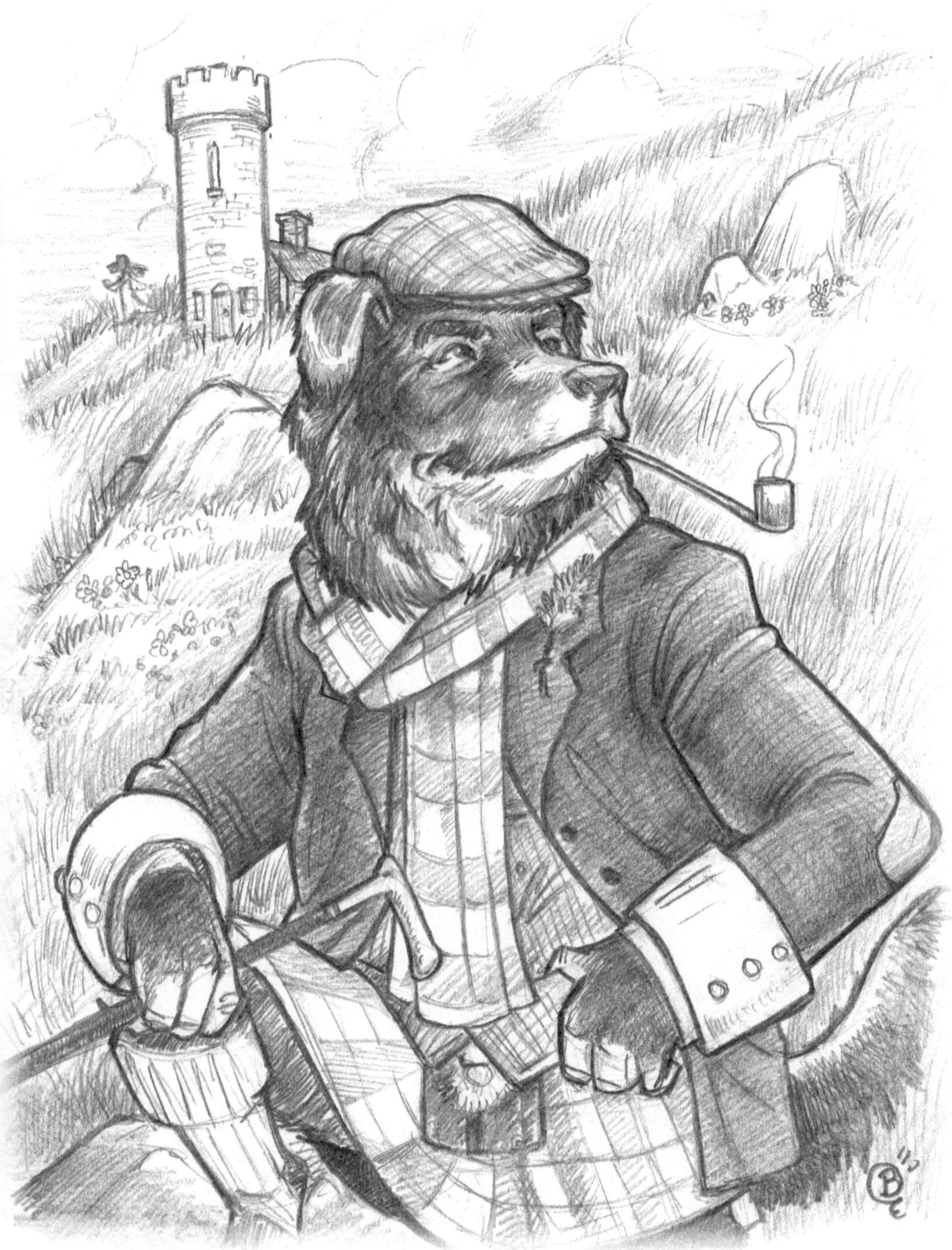

Lord Augustus Ferretish III
First Earl of Nibbleton

Augustus is the sole heir to the Ferretish fortune, a duelist, and a roguish drifter with a sense of justice. After seeing the cruelty and inequality of the world, he decided to do something about it. During the day he holds court in his stately manor, but under the shadow of night, he takes on the persona of the The Crimson Blade. Highwaymen and blaggards beware – The Crimson Blade defends the downtrodden!

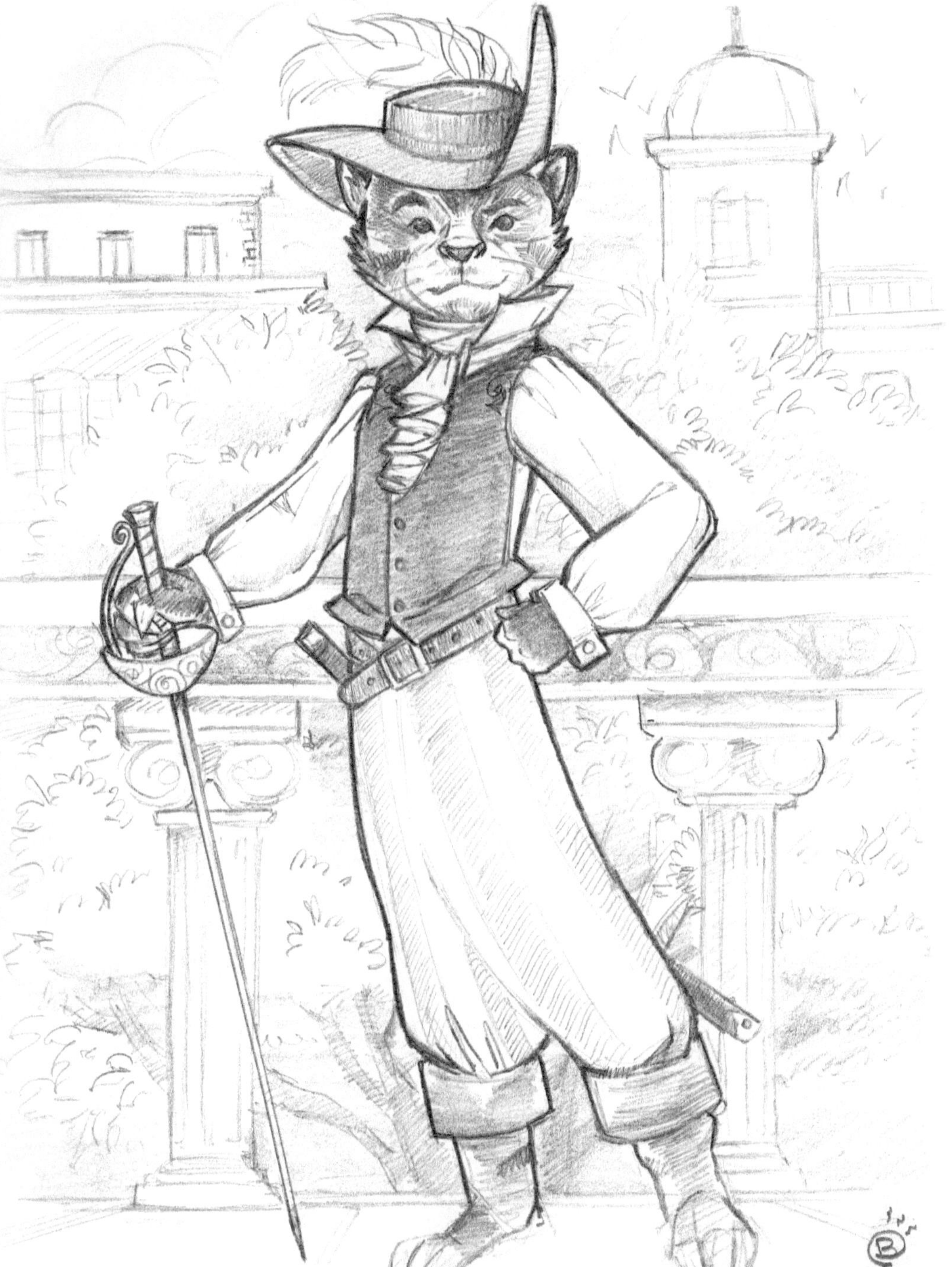

Baron Albrecht Lupashca

Not much is known about the reclusive nobleman. His generosity to the peasantry in his province is held in high esteem, and his nightly roaming of the countryside is a whispered topic of conversation.

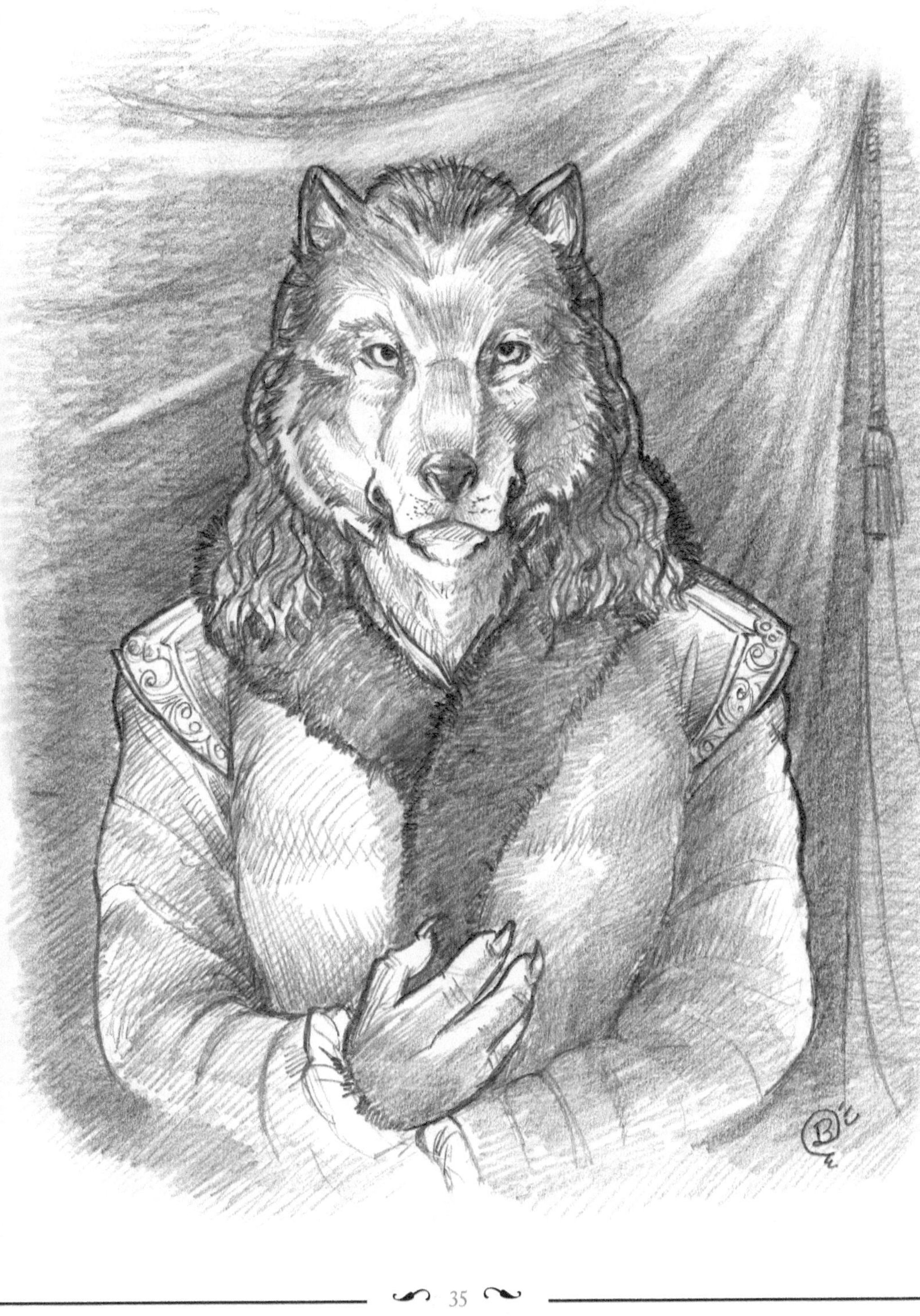

Mayor Walter Tuskerton
of Carpenters Bay

Carpenters Bay is a colorless corner of the world, filled with tough people and even tougher seas. It takes a real leader to keep this brawling town of fishermen, treasure seekers, shipwrights and hard-tack families in line, but Walther Tuskerton is up to the task. This former shoreman is a salty customer who doesn't suffer fools or trouble-makers and has been known to toss rogues into the ocean if they lay their hands on his oysters.

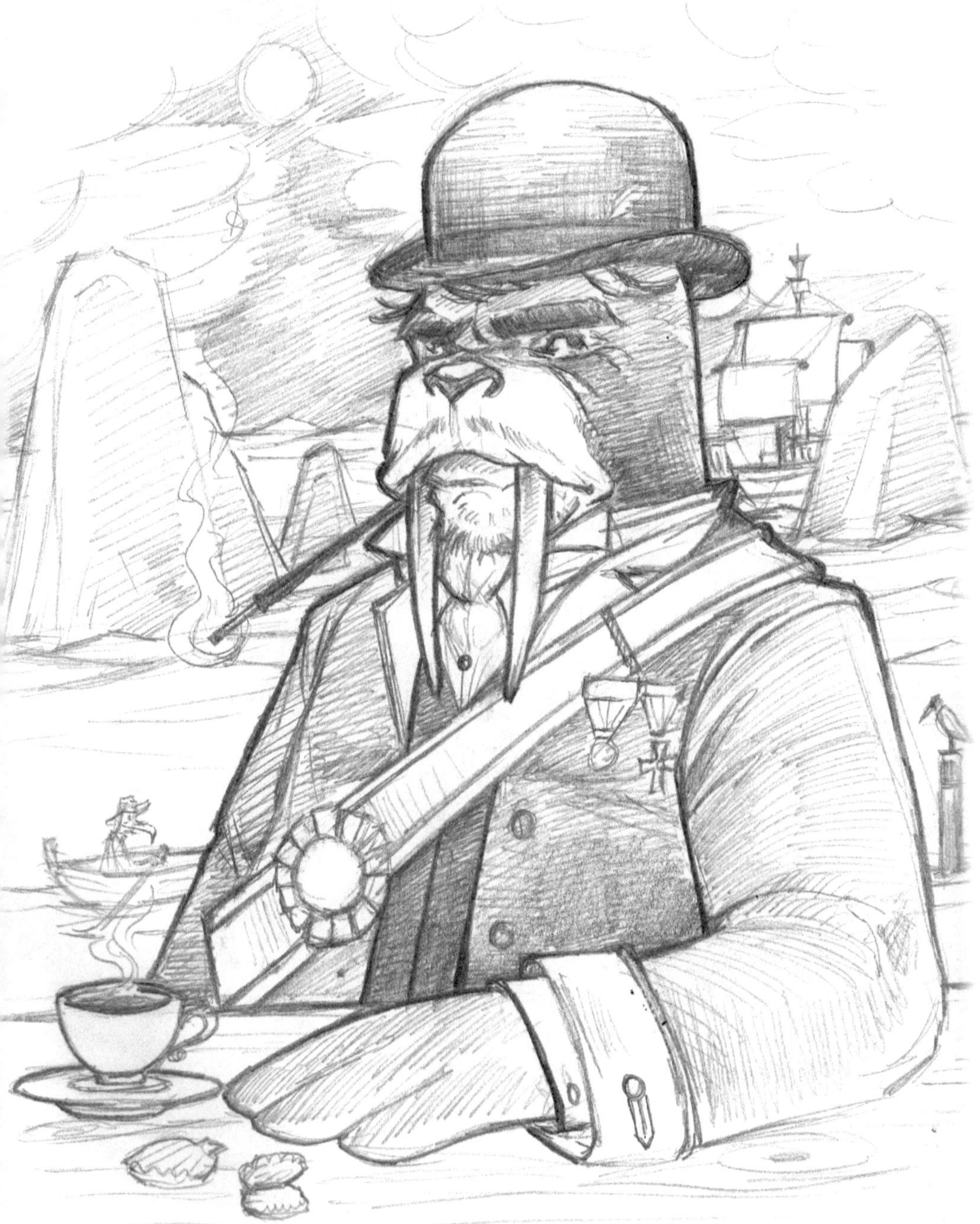

Miss Eustice Queensland

Eustice is the youngest daughter of the Queensland family and the heiress to Kaptain Koala's Premium Eucalyptus Jams and Jelly. She's considered by most to be a shy girl with a very reserved nature, especially amongst her fellow debutantes. However, she graduated from university at the tender age of fourteen and has one of the most brilliant minds in the world. She figures if she can handle advanced calculus and theoretical physics, a formal dance should be a piece of cake.

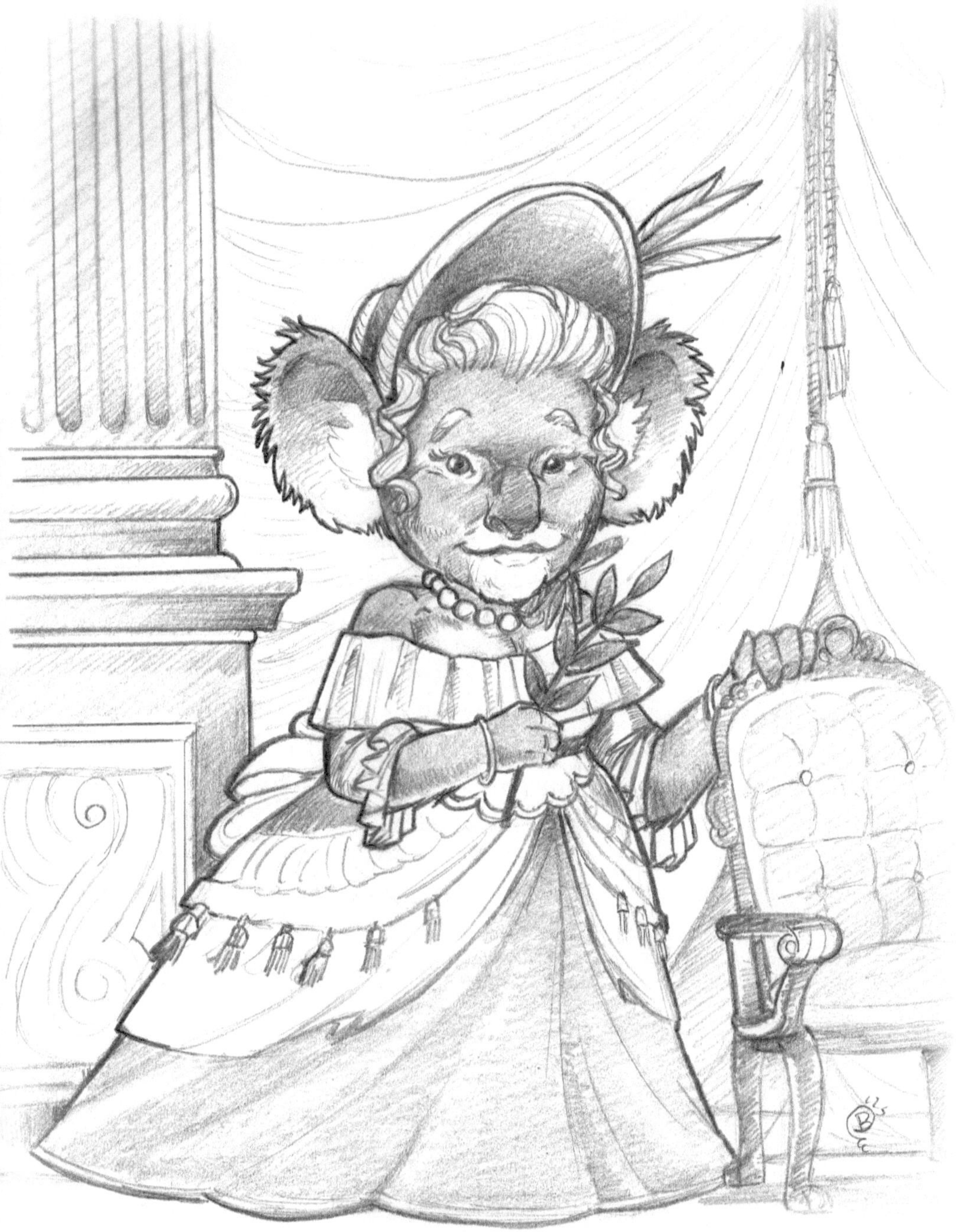

Mssr. Fabian Reynard

Born to a noble family and a small fortune, Fabian's father gambled away his inheritance before he was old enough to leave home. This would have been a major setback for most, but not Fabian. He found he had a knack for cards, dice, and slight of hand which made him perfectly suited for his future career as a world-class thief. His father would have been so proud.

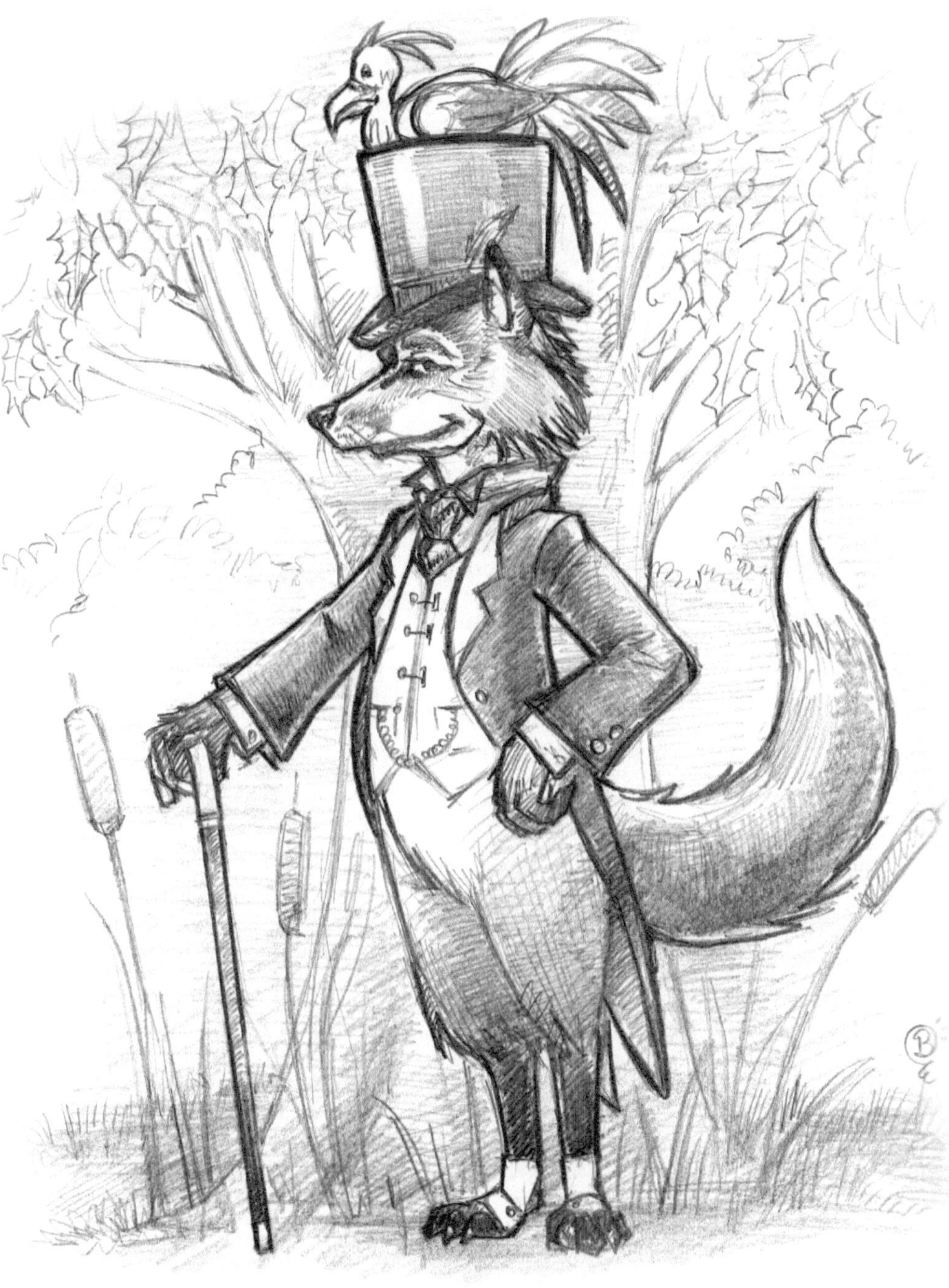

Capt. Orlando de Nutria

During the age of discovery, Captain Orlando was one of the first to strike out to discover new worlds and far off shores. Unfortunately, his path took him through the fabled Devil's Triangle. There he found a rough trip going from bad to worse. Now, almost two hundred years later, this cursed adventurer is still trying to find his way out, and his crew is obviously taking issue with navigational skills.

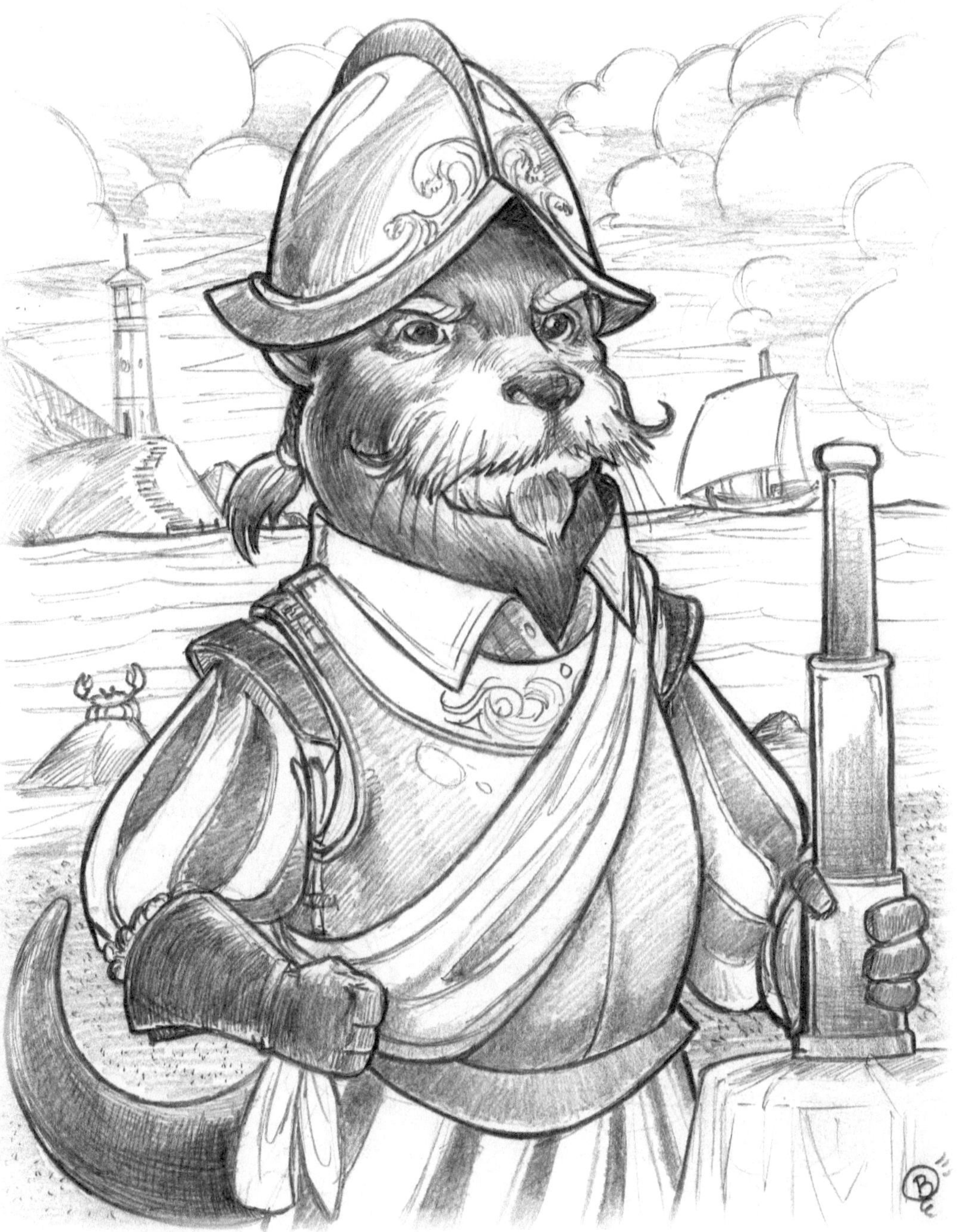

Walt William Longneck

W.W. Longneck is a big-hearted poet and writer of long-winded love letters. The sole benefactor of his great uncle's fortune, Walt has been afforded the time and leisure to pursue his writing career, such as it is. He has written three books of poetry of "questionable quality" and one stage play. One reviewer said this of his work,

"After reading W.W. Longneck's most recent compositions, I now hope that he takes up golfing and leaves poetry to the professionals."

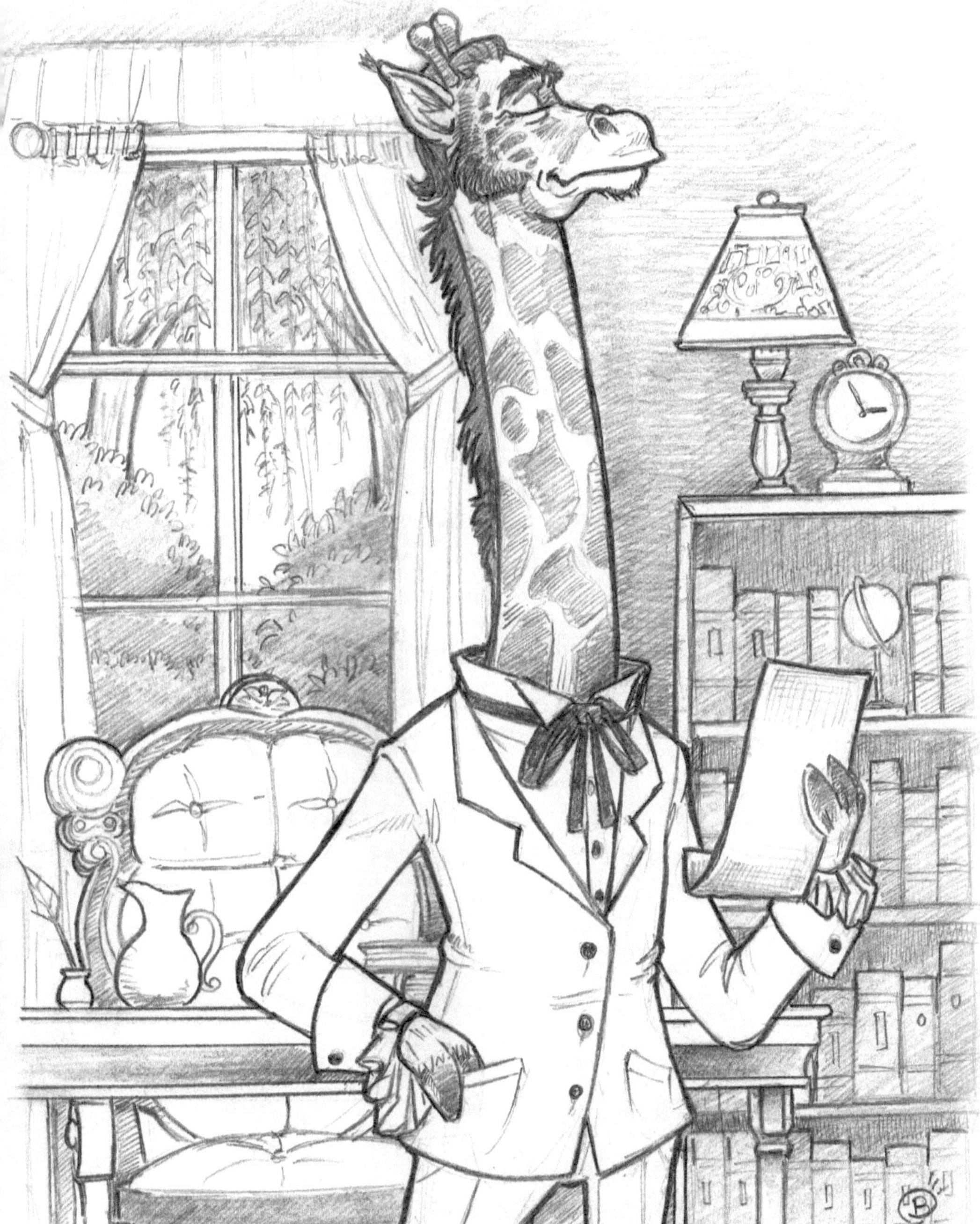

General Ravjit Gajendra

Counselor to the Maharaja, and commander of his forces, Ravjit is a calculating warrior, a fierce opponent, and (strangely enough) an incredibly sensitive musician. He is a lover of philosophy from many cultures and cultivates knowledge and wisdom amongst the soldiers in his charge. It is rumored a holy man once said that General Gajendra was the reincarnation of an ancient sadhu, or a religious ascetic. He replied, "HA! Do I look like I have the patience to be a monk? I can barely wait for my men to finish their breakfast."

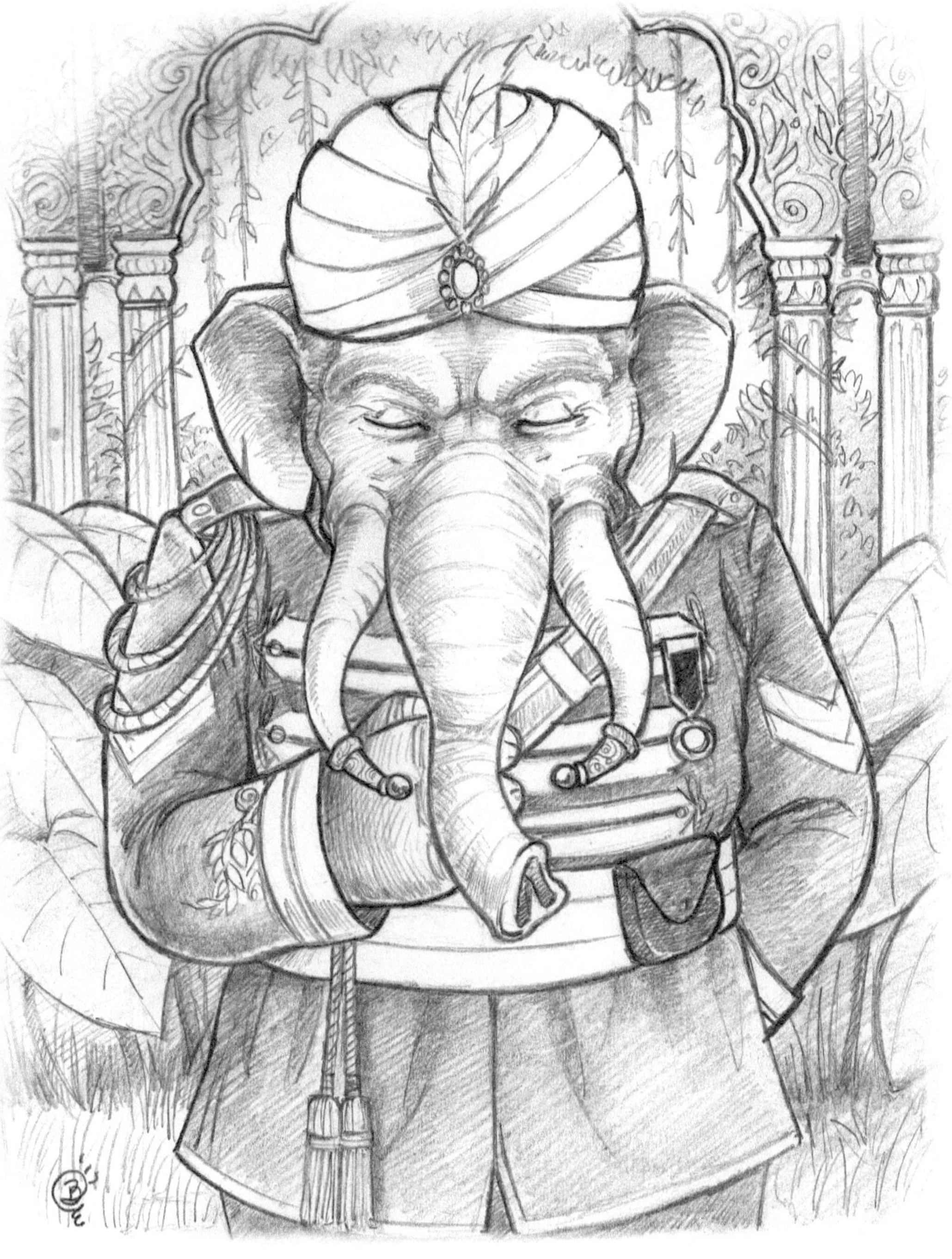

Edward Mouchard

A star of the stage and screen, Edward has played all of the best roles from Hamlet to the Phantom of the Opera. Although he is known as a talented performer, he is also a notorious lothario that has left a path of broken hearts behind him like strewn rose petals.

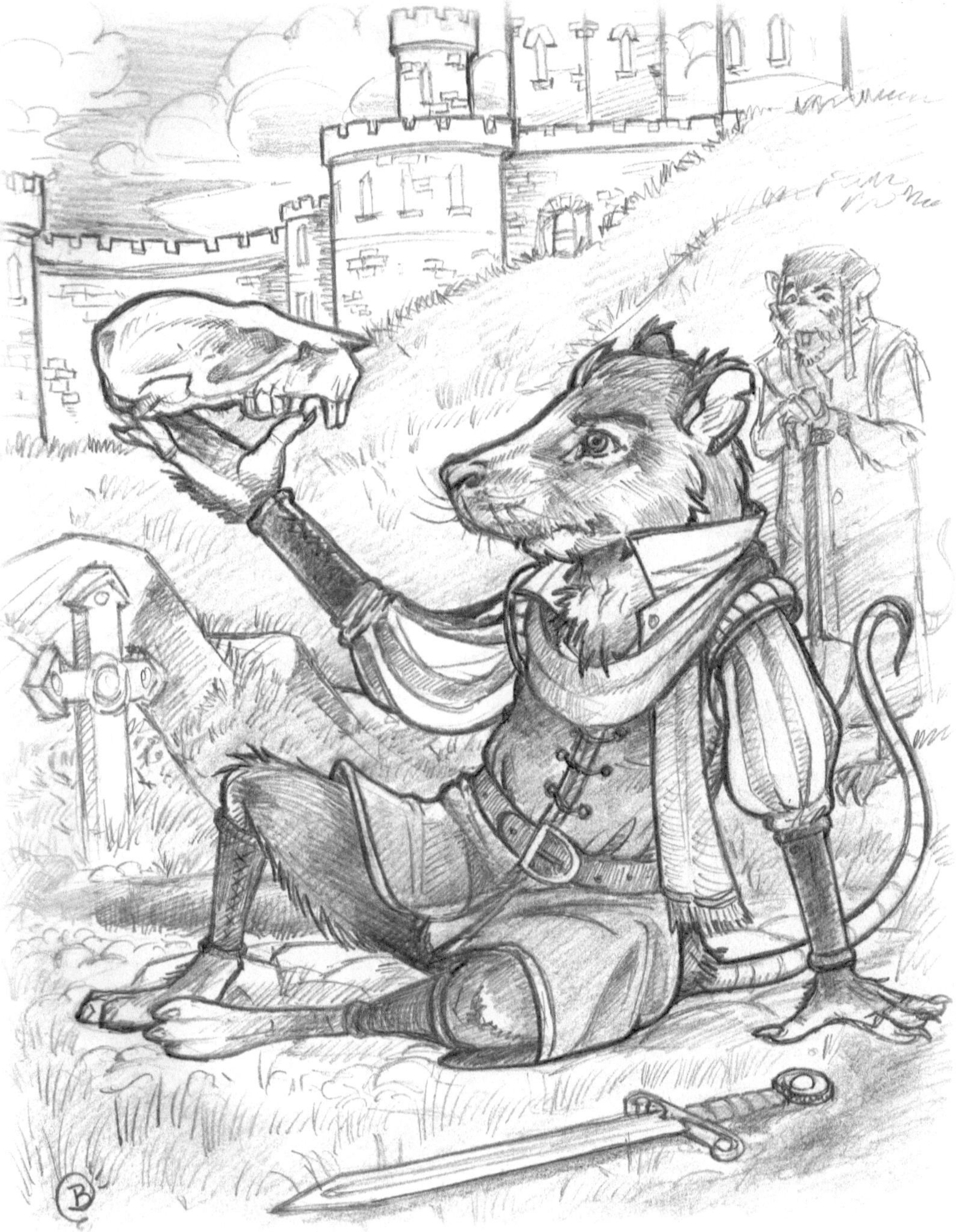

Alphonse Bubalus

Born in a small village, Alphonze was apprenticed to one of the country's most renowned painters, Marsala de Cocha. His master was bordering on insane, spending hours in his studio trying to capture the perfect painting of a bowl of rotten pears. Alphonze learned a great deal from his "dedication to his craft." Years later, now a master portrait painter, he still cringes at the sight of rotten fruit.

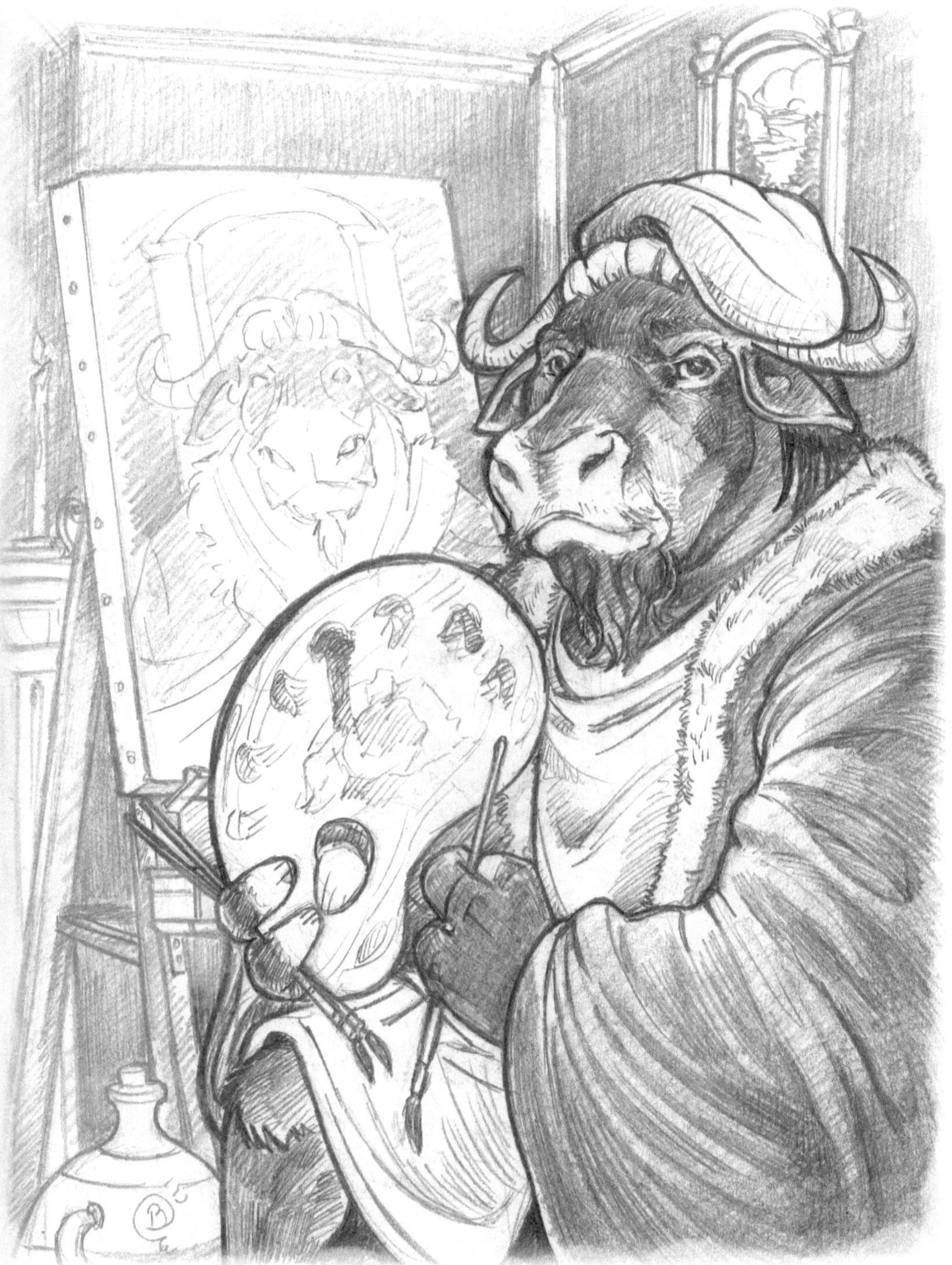

Lord Slurman Snadderly

The wheels of government turn slowly on the best of days, but when something lands on Lord Snadderly's desk, the wheels grind to screeching halt. This is one meticulous sloth, and nothing gets passed along from his purview without being checked, checked again, and triple checked. Hope you're not in a hurry to get any laws passed this year.

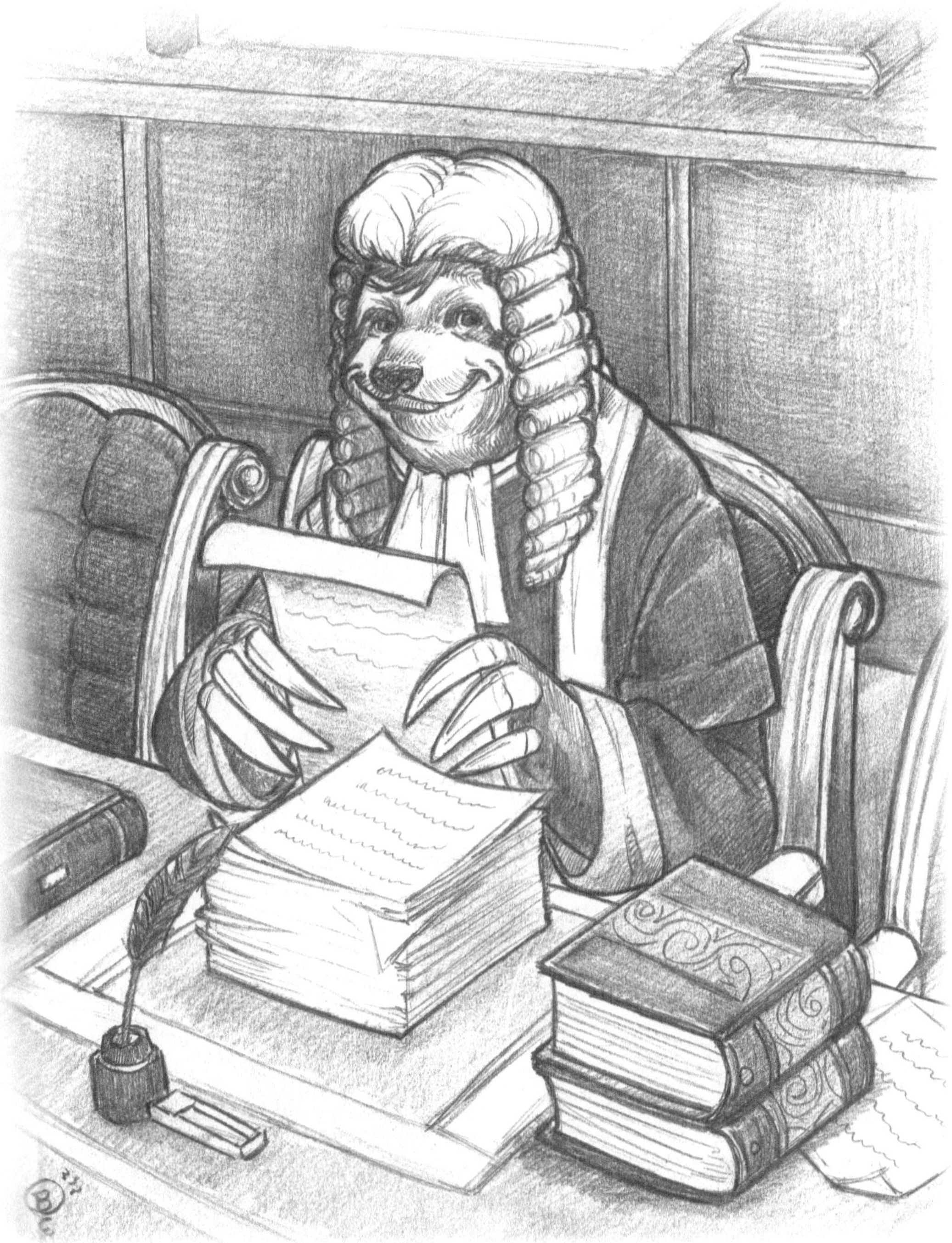

Bronagh Brockwell

The Badger's Delight is hailed as the greatest ale ever concocted by beast, and there are those that would physically fight you if you said otherwise. When Bronagh Brockwell set out to brew her famous libation, she was only trying to make something special to sell in her family's inn – little did she know that it would raise her to fame and fortune. She, her husband, and their children still own the inn and live a fairly modest life. It takes more than a little money to turn the head of a Brockwell.

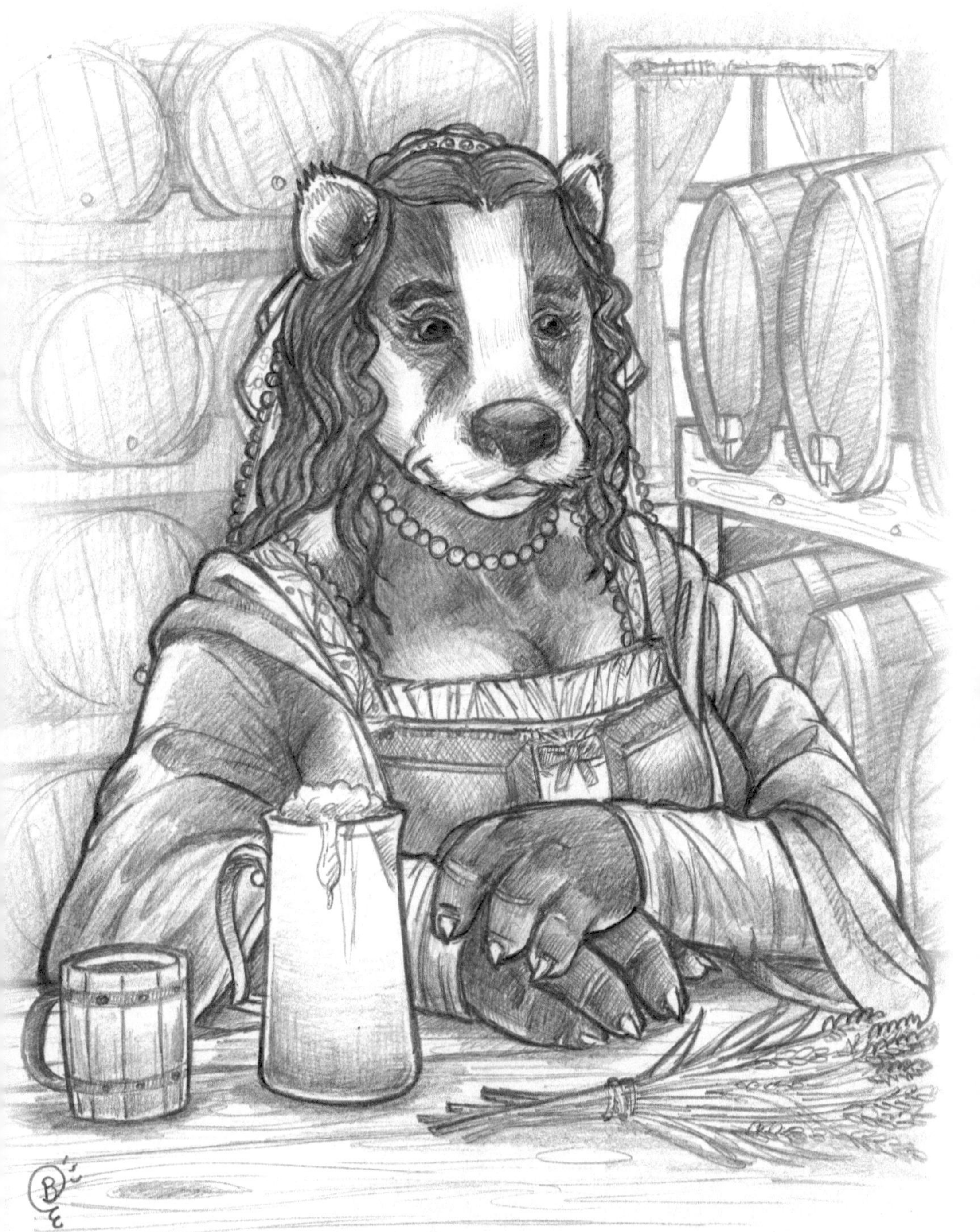

His Majesty,
King Judah Ariel Leonidas IV

The line of Leonidas has seen its fair share of despots, madmen, and milquetoast rulers. However, with the birth of Judah Ariel, the family hoped to be brought back to their former glory. His first act as king was to declare a grand holiday celebrating his favorite thing in the world – pie. Yes, Judah was just as mad as his predecessors, but you have to admit, who doesn't love pie?

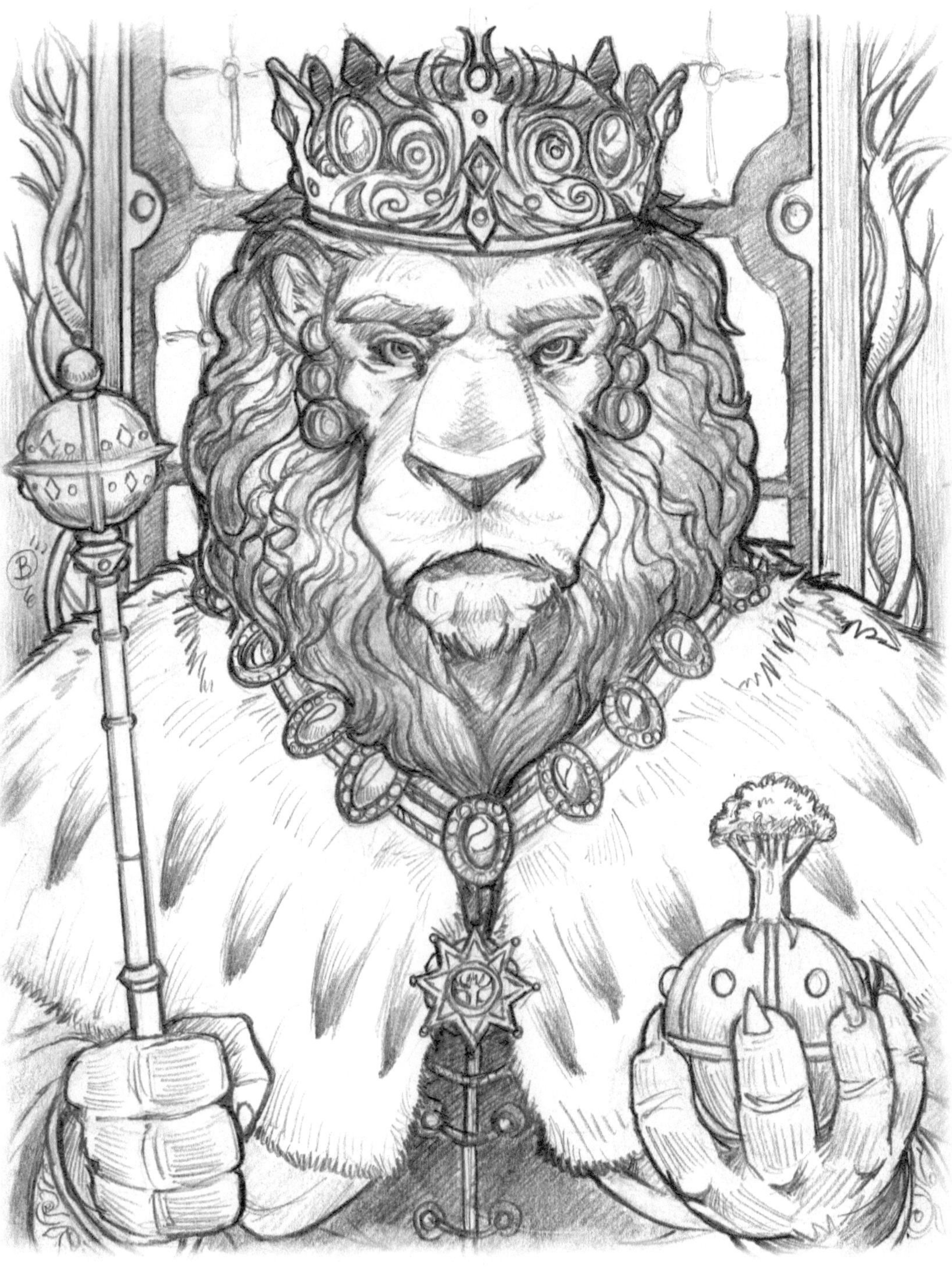

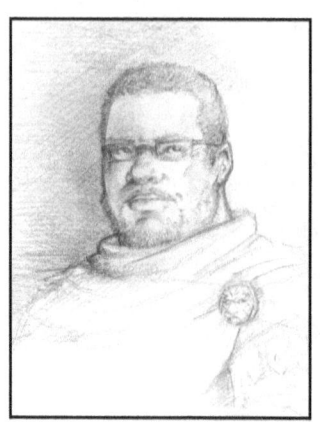

Brian W. Parker
Author, Illustrator, and Creator of the Fantastical

Brian grew up in Alaska, then Mississippi, and has always been in love with storytelling in every medium. He earned a BFA in graphic design & illustration and an MA in writing & publishing. Brian now spends his days working in youth publishing (so cool, right?) through his company, Believe In Wonder, which he co-owns with his wife, Josie. He is the author of *Crow in the Hollow*, *You Can Rely on Platypi*, and co-author of *Obi The Changeling*, *Nicholas & Sabina in The Busy Season* and *The Wonderous Science*

PICK UP THESE AMAZING BOOKS

from BELIEVE IN WONDER PUBLISHING

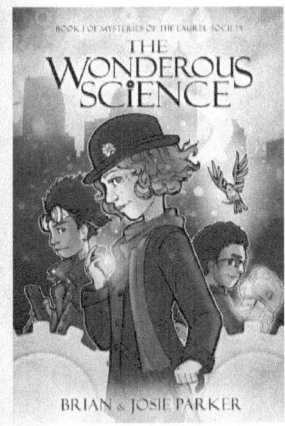
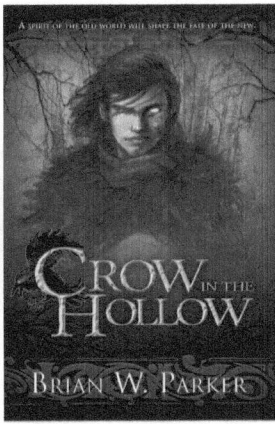
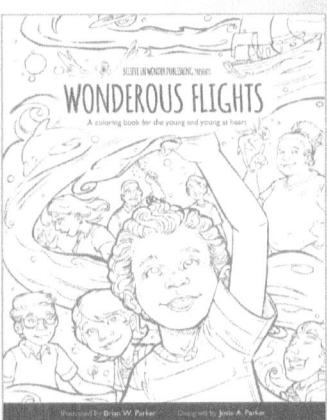
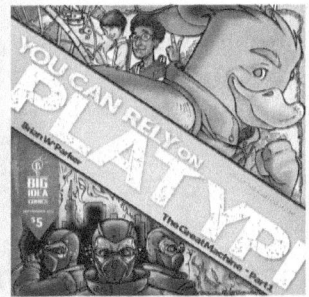
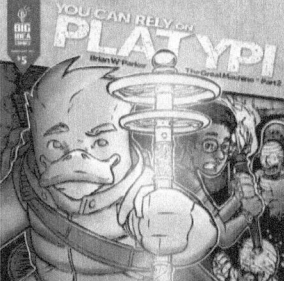
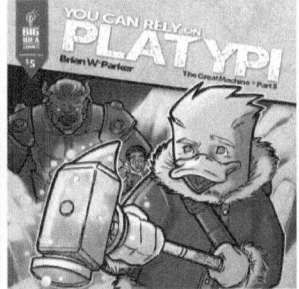
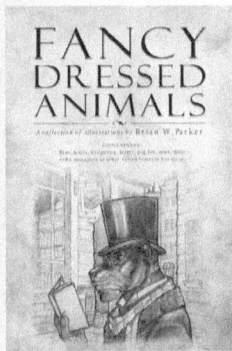
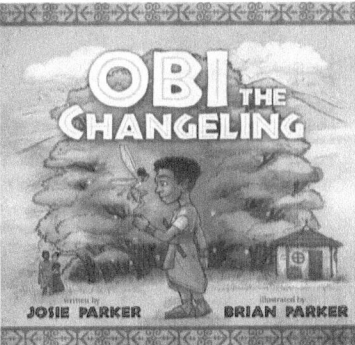
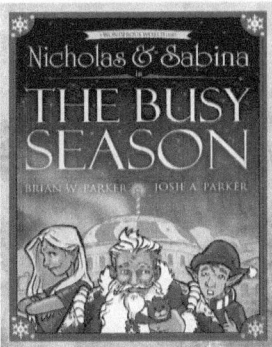

now available on AMAZON.COM

visit WWW.BELIEVEINWONDER.COM

www.ingramcontent.com/pod-product-compliance
Lightning Source LLC
Chambersburg PA
CBHW030508220526
45464CB00006B/2708